Spirit-Full Eating
Beholding the Door

Part One: The Battle

Sophia Tucker

Cover by Matthew Tucker

This book is dedicated to Samantha. When I doubted myself, your life story made me realize that if I could only help one, and you were that one, it would've all been worth it ...

Contents

Prologue 1

Introduction 9

Chapter 1 My Testimony—The Beginning.................12

Chapter 2 The Answer 22

Chapter 3 What Is Spirit-Full Eating?.........................27

Chapter 4 The Struggle..37

Chapter 5 Wait! This Has Been Going On from the Beginning? 41

Chapter 6 The Master Distracter 49

Chapter 7 The Spirit Expressly Says 60

Chapter 8 The Abundance 69

Chapter 9 The Great Takeback............................74

Chapter 10 The Fullness 79

Chapter 11 Focus on the Gift 83

Conclusion 93

Additional Information 97

Prologue

Beholding the door—the dream

I found myself on a red double-decker bus in the thick of night. The journey was unsteady, lurching jerkily down the dimly lit road, traveling with my family. They were guiding me, showing me the way, and imparting valuable lessons. Street lamps glared through the window as we meandered through the city streets. Suddenly, the bus broke down, grinding to a stop. The brakes screeched in my ears like a piercing needle. I was instructed to get off. Dazed and confused, I stumbled down the rickety steps of the old, red bus and onto the cold concrete pavement.

Leaving the stranded bus behind, I ventured into a small shopping district. The cobbled streets were uneven and old-fashioned, as if from a bygone era, swallowed up in the heart of this metropolis. To my dismay, all the shops were strangely boarded up, leaving the place eerily desolate.

Undeterred, I sought refuge in a dank alley under a bridge. As I ventured deeper into the dimly lit alley, shuffling my feet forward nervously, every sense and sound was heightened in the darkness. I constantly felt I was being watched.

Then, emerging into view from the shadows ahead, a group of hostile men confronted me, hurling taunts, objects, and punches my way. Overwhelmed, I found myself being thrown down a steep slope into a basement. I didn't remember the journey of how I ended up there, but I knew I was trapped with seemingly no escape.

I surveyed my prison. Inside the poorly lit basement, a bothersome leak from the roof dripped in the background. It made the odor musty and claustrophobic.

I wasn't alone. I encountered a few individuals seeking solace from the harsh world above. Then, to my surprise, two women with warm smiles appeared, bearing bags of food. My gratitude for the food was overshadowed by the knowledge that it consisted of foods that I was reluctant to eat—a diet I was warned against for its supposed negative health effects. I felt I had no choice but to accept the food while in captivity.

The passage of time was marked by a significant event—the arrival of Christmas. Having gotten used to the place, the room seemed lighter now. While we were allowed some guests, the captors relished their Christmas lunch above ground. We remained in the basement, celebrating Christmas with modest food, activities, and music.

In this confined space, I met a young woman juggling four degrees, stretched thin, and contemplating her true desires. I also had a heartfelt conversation with another young woman whose parents generously supported her studies—a stark contrast to the first lady, who was struggling to finance her education alone.

Moved by compassion, we devised a plan for both women to escape their captivity. Encouraged, the young girl who struggled with finances took matters into her own hands by setting a fire as a diversion. During the chaos, we became aware that our keepers had been purposely feeding us special food in order to distract us from our captivity.

While the fire caused confusion upstairs, the two women and I seized the opportunity to run and run, finally escaping the clutches of our captors. We were met by a door that had an opening button to press on our side for our escape.

As we went through the door and reached the outside, we came to a gated area where a man, who was the heavenly figure of Christ, stood in an opening. His sparkling eyes dazzled with compassion.

We frantically ran around in a yellow-sanded confined space, trying to find a way to Him, only to realize that, all along, the door had been wide open for us to walk out. As we hurriedly did so, we sprinted toward the man at the door and reached Him and His wide-open arms of freedom.

An interpretation

I had this vivid dream repeatedly and, over the years, the Holy Spirit has unraveled its deeper meaning.

It symbolized my vulnerability, how I was entrapped by the enemy's deception, and bound to an unhealthy relationship with food—a false comfort and support. I was completely wrapped up in the wrong view of health at the time.

In the dream, the two ladies and I together represented the trinity of my being—spirit, soul, and body. We found balance with Jesus by working together, leading toward escape. My spirit offered counsel to my soul, which was burdened by a sense of orphanhood, and striving to fulfill noble, yet natural desires.

In this dream, I discovered that Christ had been ever-present, standing at the door of my heart, waiting to guide me to freedom. The door was now clear. I needed to open it, and the door opener was on my side.

The goal was to commune with Him, and to seek answers within, rather than running around searching elsewhere. He alone wanted to sit with me, to walk through all the parts of my soul and body, and to help me discover freedom. This revelation is not just for me. This is available to everyone—a path toward liberation and communion with God.

The Lord gave me these verses that described my dream:

> Those whom I [dearly and tenderly] love, I rebuke and discipline [showing them their faults and instructing them]; so be enthusiastic and repent [change your inner self—your old way of thinking, your sinful behavior—seek God's will]. Behold, I stand at the door [of the church] and continually knock. If anyone hears My voice and opens the door, I will

come in and eat with him (restore him), and he with Me. He
who overcomes [the world through believing that Jesus is the
Son of God], I will grant to him [the privilege] to sit beside
Me on My throne, as I also overcame and sat down beside My
Father on His throne. He who has an ear, let him hear and
heed what the Spirit says to the churches.
— Revelation 3:9, 20–22 AMPC

God was calling me to behold the door, to hear His voice
calling me, to open to Him, and to allow His restoration to
heal me and set me free.

The key to Spirit-Full Eating is communing with Him. We
open the door, let Him in, and sit with Him. We eat, drink,
and go through our daily lives with Him. It reminds me of this
verse:

Repeat them again and again to your children. Talk about
them when you are at home and when you are on the road,
when you are going to bed and when you are getting up. Tie
them to your hands and wear them on your forehead as
reminders. Write them on the doorposts of your house and on
your gates.
— Deuteronomy 6:7–9 NLT

This is not only a well-known verse for parenting, but also
a reminder that wherever we go and whatever we do, we are
to be meditating on the truths and promises of God's Word.
All parts of our beings—our spirits, souls, and bodies—have
doors. These doors allow the glory of God to flow through to
all parts of our beings, transforming us from the inside out. As

we are the temple and house of God, the Word of God will heal and restore us in every area so we can be preserved blameless.

> Now may the God of peace make you holy in every way, and may your whole spirit and soul and body be kept blameless until our Lord Jesus Christ comes again. God will make this happen, for he who calls you is faithful.
> — 1 Thessalonians 5:23 NLT

This dream was a wake-up call to my own deception at the time, but was also just the beginning of my discovering how to walk with Him for life, health, and godliness.

And, so, I have embarked on a lifelong practice of Spirit-Full Eating—a journey of feasting on true food and true drink, a journey of fellowship and communion with Him.

No longer seeking answers in worldly wisdom, I have surrendered everything at His feet. I've embraced His truth and found His salvation in my heart, soul, mind, and body. I've experienced healing my dark places, and rejuvenation in my weakened areas. I've discovered wholeness. I am finally free.

The door to freedom opened, and I stepped into His courts, filled with thanksgiving and praise. Shackles that once bound me have fallen away. I've begun a glorious mass exodus—my personal coming-out-of-Egypt story. I've entered the rich Promised Land, a place abundant in flowing milk and honey, and I've been liberated from narrowness.

On this journey, God has called me to be separate, and to stand out as His chosen one, ready to embrace all He has in store.

This dream set me on my journey of revelation and divine communion, the story of my transformation into a soul liberated by God's grace and love.

I am beholding the door to the way, the truth, and life—Jesus. Let us behold Him together.

Beholding the Door

Amidst life's journey, a door awaits,
Are you prepared to step through the gate?
Behold the entrance, His pathway divine,
Close the door behind, as you say, "His will becomes mine."

His courts of grace, where praises resound,
Where thanksgiving's symphony is always found.
Farewell to chains that held us tight,
Embrace His freedom, bathed in His light.

With an attentive ear, Holy Spirit calls,
Let His wisdom within you truly enthrall.
Listen, and hear His sacred voice,
Guiding you beyond the noise.

A door of wonder beckons near,
Will you answer His call without fear?
He will unveil the truths that were once concealed,
Discover the truth He longs to reveal.

In His Holy Communion, you find the key,
Unlocking treasures to become free.
So, heed the whispers, soft and clear,
A new chapter of life now appears.

Introduction

How This Book Works

This book is part one of a three-part series on Spirit-Full Eating. To get the most out of it, reflectively read each chapter with the Lord, and then proactively journal with Him. There are some sections in the chapters to help with this.

Scripture references

At the beginning of each chapter the verses used are listed. Take these verses and meditate on them.

Recap and reflect

This is your time for personal reflection and for devotion to the Lord, to help you delve deeper. The end of each chapter includes a recap of the main points discussed and some thought-provoking questions. These can also be used in small groups or church fellowship.

A biblical affirmation or prayer

The affirmations are solely based on the verses in the Bible and what the Lord has shown me through them. Regularly meditate on these and read the prayer.

You may find it helpful to follow along with our Spirit-Full Eating Journal, and the online Bible study and classes available from September 2023 (see the additional information section at the end of the book for the links).

This book is not just words on a page. It is an opportunity for deeper reflection and life application. How many books have you read? How many studies have you completed? How much have you retained? And how much are you living out?

To shut down the voices of other programs and plans, and all unnecessary noise, pause and reflect often to hear the Spirit as you read this book. I hope you will come away from reading it with new insights and revelations from the Lord.

You may need to read this book multiple times to receive, digest, and walk out all God has for you.

The topic of Spirit-Full Eating is a vast subject and so it is split into volumes. This first volume explains the principles and heart of Spirit-Full Eating.

Please follow us at Tapestry of Beauty Ministries and Spirit-Full Eating for more teachings, mind renewal kits, and programs as they are released (all the links are in the additional information section of the book).

Disclaimer

Please note that this is not a call to throw out your medication, to not go to your doctor's appointments, or to stop anything that you have been directed to do by a doctor as the Lord has led you. The work we are doing here is internal, first and foremost.

Chapter 1
My Testimony—The Beginning

Scripture references

Colossians 2:20–23; 3 John 1:2; Psalms 23:1–3; Ephesians 1:18

Like many others, I grew up with a negative view of my body because I did not grow up with the Lord in my life. My confidence was minimal, and I struggled with my identity. Fast forward to my twenties, I met the Lord and was radically saved. And so, my journey of healing began. Praise the Lord, I was formally introduced to Jesus. He picked me up. Never mentioned my weight, and started teaching me about a love that I had never before experienced.

My weight was stable at first, but it still was being maintained by cycles of eating and restricting. I then became more focused on the Lord and being consumed with Him, rather than with weight and food. My weight slowly started to creep up, but I had peace.

In hindsight, I wish I had stayed in this place and allowed the Lord to change me from the inside out. But comments started, and around the corner was my wedding to my soon-to-be, wonderful husband. No bride can be plump, right? So, I went on yet another strict plan to lose weight. I was then near my lowest weight but, even on my wedding day, I felt insecure and cringed at the beautiful pictures I now see today. Dieting continued with babies and, yes, I am sad to say that happened even during pregnancies and breastfeeding.

I knew I loved Jesus, and I really wanted to find how to do it His way. I then discovered and settled on a few ministers who taught that by renewing your mind you could lose weight and not turn to food for emotional reasons. This revolutionized my view of food at the time, and I am forever grateful for their wisdom. I also learned that renewing my mind was the key to getting me out of depression and anxiety. It was the answer that led to me writing my first book, *Renewing the Mind 101*, teaching the principles of God's view of a changed life.

My obsession with food and binge eating didn't fully end, however, and I had to find a new path with the help of the Word. My emotional eating was healed through learning to give my emotions, stress, and triggers to God through renewing my mind.

I had finally broken free from the bondage of emotional eating once I realized it was never really about the food! It was about my walk with Jesus. It was often about so many other matters going on in my life and how I handled them.

God told me I could eat emotionally since we all have difficult emotions, but instead of turning to natural food and drink to cope, to rather draw from Him as my true food and drink.

My journey continued this way for several years. Until God told me to stop dieting. I then struggled with a reluctance to stop for two or three years. I was addicted to boundaries, dieting, and programs. After all, I wanted to honor God with my body, and I thought that keeping boundaries and following programs was the way I truly honored the Lord.

The next shift in my transformation journey came when I went deeper into my identity in Christ. Game changer. However, when I finally decided to give up food restrictions and programs, I still struggled with the diet mindset, which led me to continue to dip in and out of other wellness plans.

My confusion came when I thought I heard the Lord say *only* eat the foods I have made. At the time, I thought this meant that God was telling me to only eat the foods found in nature, absolutely nothing processed or tampered with. I interpreted this harshly: If I didn't eat this way, there would be serious consequences. Therefore, because of a diet mindset, I saw this from a restrictive perspective and tried to enforce this supposed rule as yet another diet.

God would repeatedly tell me that dieting, scales, all of it, were a cultural mindset that was driving my decisions and passions. This was clouding the fear of the Lord in my life; instead of being directed by Him, I still had some areas of my mind that needed to be renewed.

My decisions had to instead come from the Lord, meditation on the awesomeness of God, and being in awe of His majesty.

I had to once again deeply surrender to the leading of the Spirit and to His guidance in every area of my life. The Lord led me to write down every diet I had been on and every food concept I had believed, and this consumed so many pages. This exercise helped me to identify patterns of behavior that were destructive and led by the flesh, rather than by the Spirit.

I had a big wake-up call when I realized that God didn't say, "Eat only the foods I have made" in the tone I had assumed it to be. At this point, the Lord revealed to me that how I had heard was incorrect. It broke me.

Because of the restrictive mindset that I held at the time, I had interpreted "Eat the foods I have made" as including an "only." This misdirected my understanding of what God had said.

My healing journey taught me that the Lord was saying that I may eat freely, focusing on the abundance of the goodness He has created for me in nature. My personal experience, my own invitation from the Lord, is that the main basis of my meals is foods made by the Lord. This is not a rule, but an opportunity to connect with my Father's beautiful creation. I also eat foods like cake, chocolate, and candy, and they are not morally wrong or bad.

I learned that God has created healing foods for us, and that His creation is amazing.

I discovered that when our hearts are tender toward Him, we will receive His direction without confusion.

I had to realize that all decisions and plans outside of the Holy Spirit are vain attempts at self-righteousness. I had to give Him a clean slate to work with, with *no food rules or diet laws*. It was the only way.

> Therefore, if you died with Christ from the basic principles of the world, why, as though living in the world, do you subject yourselves to regulations—"Do not touch, do not taste, do not handle," which all concern things which perish with the using—according to the commandments and doctrines of men? These things indeed have an appearance of wisdom in self-imposed religion, false humility, and neglect of the body, but are of no value against the indulgence of the flesh.
> — Colossians 2:20–23 NKJV

God taught me those diet laws created by people and well-meaning Christians are not from Him. Yep! Dieting is a natural method of trying to fix and solve a spiritual need. You see, God began to teach me that someone's external appearance or weight does not determine health. What we call health is not what God calls it. And how we go about it is not always what He believes is best for us.

He tells us that He wills for us to prosper and to be in health *as our souls prosper*. He teaches us that He is the answer to health. Health is as described here:

> Beloved, I pray that you may prosper in all things and be in
> health, just as your soul prospers.
> — 3 John 1:2 NKJV

Health is not just in the body—it's the mind and heart and imagination, and so much more.

On my journey to healing there were tears, confusion, struggles, and fears—things that had been buried deep within me revived themselves.

But it was okay because I was doing this with the Lord, and He is patient and faithful to His promises. The Lord wasn't doing this because I was a hot mess and He just had to have mercy on me, but because, I realized, He loves me and enjoys partnering with me. It's beautiful.

Having a baby in 2022 taught me to surrender my health again, and His miracle-working hands were evident in keeping me, my body, and my daughter throughout the pregnancy. I decided that I would not allow my weight to stop me from having another baby as promised by the Lord and that He would keep us—and He did!

Today I am healed from a diet mentality and I am now walking with the Holy Spirit in my everyday decisions. These choices are now rather about how I can discover Him more, about our unity and oneness, and less about food—and definitely not an obsession with weight loss or weight gain. My binge eating days are behind me. Emotional eating? Gone!

I appreciate food a lot more. I am learning new things about my body and appetite daily, and I love it. The Lord leads me as needed on food and movement, very, very gently, one step at a time. I am purposefully on a joyful, amazing, and gentle process of relearning and training my senses. But the unlearning is complete.

My day is focused on God's heart. What do we get to do today? What's on Your heart today? Sometimes, what shall I eat today? He leads me gently, with joy, and with no food rules, focusing on taking in beneficial and healing foods and enjoying all other foods too. Teaching me how, together with Him, to honor and love His temple. And how to train my children to not fall into the same traps I did.

> The Lord is my shepherd; I shall not want. He makes me lie down in green pastures. He leads me beside still waters. He restores my soul. He leads me in paths of righteousness for his name's sake.
> — Psalms 23:1–3 ESV

God gave me permission to eat! Even though at times it was scary at first. Somewhere down the line, certain foods lost their thrill and obsession. I knew who I was in Him and what He had for me. My mindset was not consumed with food. My heart and mind were set on my one thing, my one desire—Him!

My journey continues, and it's amazing. I realize that God has provided the gift of His creation for our benefit. He has changed my desires to see the wonder in His creation of foods and nature, and how it is His will for me to enjoy all of His rich bounty. I am not mastered by any food or group, all is permissible. But He has also shown me that the most beneficial is *love* and that everything I do, or eat, or drink is governed by my love relationship with Him. His statement of, "Only eat the foods I have made" has now transformed into, "Only love Me, and then you will love what I suggest for you, what I have made and provided for you."

I invite you on this journey with me, as we walk out of the prison gates and into the glorious freedom God has for us.

Recap and reflect

- From my journey you will see how I went back and forth with my health journey. I truly struggled to fully surrender all my cares to the Lord. Have you turned your health journey over to the Lord?

- My mind was bombarded with so many insights from well-meaning friends, family, and the media. What messages have you received about the body, food, and health?

- Knowing how you got here and why you want to change is so important. What is your why for wanting to walk in freedom?

- I shared how I found that I had been addicted to programs. I believe it was a form of me trying to control things, but also because I just did not know how to find the answer to long-lasting health. Have you ever considered that you could have been addicted to diets? Or other wellness plans or programs? What is your history with dieting?

- Many of us hold off on doing life because we are waiting for the perfect size, body, and weight. Have you been holding back on life? Avoiding events, life decisions, and being obedient to God?

- Have you ever thought you received direction from the Lord, and you perceived it from an old, destructive mindset?

- In whatever you do in the name of health, are you being led beside quiet waters (Psalm 23)? Is your soul being restored? Do you sense the peace of the Lord and the fruit of freedom in your daily walk with Christ?

Prayer

Dear Lord, as I begin this journey of trusting You for my health, open the eyes of my understanding so that I can truly comprehend all the wisdom You have for me. Help me to reflect on my own journey and the glorious future You have for me. I come to You today surrendered to Your will and purposes in my life. In Jesus' name. Amen.

> I pray that your hearts will be flooded with light so that you can understand the confident hope he has given to those he called—his holy people who are his rich and glorious inheritance.
> — Ephesians 1:18 NLT

Chapter 2
The Answer

Scripture references

Matthew 11:28–30; Matthew 19:26; 1 Corinthians 10:31; Proverbs 3:5–6

Over the years I have been in ministry, I have witnessed the struggle of many trying to not only get well, but also to stay well.

It is time we, once and for all, put to an end this seemingly endless struggle with weight and body image, false identities, and the tireless journey of dieting.

As a wife of a healing evangelist and pastor, I, together with my husband, have spent many years ministering to those with sicknesses and diseases, and we praise God for His mighty hand and miracles. My heart has been to help maintain health God's way and to prevent the many struggles we needlessly bear.

For years I had been looking for "the answer" to lose weight, and before I was a Christian I resorted to the secular diets and programs that were the most popular at the time. These programs often included strict regimes and caused an onslaught of disordered eating.

Then, as I became a Christian, I looked for a biblical approach, but many of the programs were still riddled with restrictions and rules, and basically meant living from the outside in. I also found myself caught up in "wellness plans" laced with pretenses and false claims that ended up just being another diet disguised as something Christian.

Venturing on in my own healing journey, God has shown me what His heart for my health is. He was so patient with me in my failures and in my mistakes. His continuous gentleness wooed me into crying out for the desire of His heart for me, which is divine health and healing through communion and intimacy. Allowing the Lord to direct my health decisions and lifestyle has become a driving force in me.

This isn't about losing some arbitrary amount of weight, then thanking God only for a brief minute, and then spending the rest of the time glorifying some diet program or the boundaries and strict rules (or even gentle rules) that we kept in our own strength.

I wanted nothing less than for God to get 100 percent of the glory.

> So whether you eat or drink or whatever you do, do it all for
> the glory of God.
> — 1 Corinthians 10:31 NKJV

My life is a testimony of His goodness, and not only do I want the freedom that Christ purchased for me for myself ... but also for every woman, man, and child who struggles with eating, low body esteem, disordered eating, health issues, emotional eating, and the list continues.

I am here to shout from the rooftops through this book and all the materials at my disposal, to let you know something: total freedom *is* possible.

Christ is the answer. He has always been the answer.

By living from the Spirit, with the Word and teachings of our counselor the Holy Spirit, we find the individual plan He has for each of us.

This book lays out the foundational principles that are remarkably the same for everyone. Our anchor verse for this entire book is:

> Be in health and prosper as indeed your soul prospers.
> — 3 John 1:2 NKJV

God wants you to prosper in health, but the prerequisite for this is your soul prospering.

Throughout this book and future series of resources, I will share with you the journey the Lord has taken me on (and I still am on). A journey where I have broken the strongholds and deceptions of the enemy, where I have trained my senses through love-based obedience, and have walked out my healing in faith—guiding you on how to do the same.

This is not a diet; I am not going to tell you what to eat—that is the Holy Spirit's job (Proverbs 3:5–6). This, in fact, is not about diets (apart from busting the myths of those that keep us bound), nor is it your traditional secular wellness plan. This is the discovery and application of the Holy Spirit's strategy for total health.

My friend, when we do this, there is no law, there is no diet, and there is nothing else we need. Exciting, isn't it? So, if you're ready to jump in with me, I am excited to see your own breakthrough.

It's time the Body of Christ gave Him all the glory for the mighty rebuilding of His temple, so that we can walk in divine health.

> Come to Me, all you who labor and are heavy-laden and overburdened, and I will cause you to rest. [I will ease and relieve and refresh your souls.]
> Take My yoke upon you and learn of Me, for I am gentle (meek) and humble (lowly) in heart, and you will find rest (relief and ease and refreshment and recreation and blessed quiet) for your souls.
> For My yoke is wholesome (useful, good—not harsh, hard, sharp, or pressing, but comfortable, gracious, and pleasant), and My burden is light and easy to be borne.
> — Matthew 11:28–30 AMPC

Recap and reflect

- What if we could truly trust Him 100 percent for our health, weight, and other concerns? What if we could not only receive health from the Lord, but keep it also? What would that look like? Ask yourself: Is this possible? Yes! All things are possible with God (Matthew 19:26).

- I spoke about how the gentleness of the Lord led me to freedom. Have you experienced the voice of gentleness and the goodness of God before? How would this relate to your healing and health?

- At this stage we are still learning the principles of Spirit-Full Eating. What are your fears or concerns? What are your expectations? Give these to the Lord today.

Chapter 3
What Is Spirit-Full Eating?

Scripture references
Matthew 6:21–33; Colossians 2:2–4;
2 Corinthians 4:6–7, 11:3

Spirit-Full Eating is about reconnecting with the leadership of the Holy Spirit in our spirits, all the way through to our souls and bodies. It is a process of feasting on what God defines as true food and drink, in order to find healing and His direction for divine health.

We have spent too long focusing on health from an outside perspective—through dieting, weight loss, or trying to change our bodies outside of seeing ourselves in Christ.

When we listen to our unrenewed thoughts that say we need a particular food or a type of health plan outside of Christ's will, it brings with it a distraction. This creates an idol that takes our focus off aligning our souls and bodies with the Spirit.

We have become complacent and comfortable in today's age of abundant information and opinions on health. We no longer need to truly lean on the Lord as we could turn to

Google and, within seconds, search how to improve our health, or how to lose twenty pounds by this summer.

Having knowledge, and even revelation, without the fear of the Lord and His wisdom on knowing what information to apply or not to our life choices creates a dangerous situation. We can open ourselves up to confusion and years of endless searching for the perfect answer.

We have the perfect answer, and His name is Jesus Christ.

Our goal with Spirit-Full Eating is to get back to the truths God has for us.

The danger I have seen in the church is trying to hear from the Lord to lead us into healthy habits, all the while still being mentally programmed by a destructive diet culture. Unfortunately, this means that our (unrenewed) minds can trick us into distorting truths. Even if God is trying to direct us, our minds cannot help but turn what God is saying into a diet that ultimately moves its focus away from the Spirit.

I experienced this when God advised me to eat a certain way, but my mind was caught up in a diet mentality, so I could not help but misinterpret what He was saying as something more complicated.

I will never forget when the Lord reminded me that this is much easier than we are all making it.

So what is the key?

Through the Word and seeking a deep change of heart and understanding, we begin to discover that the Spirit alone is our teacher and counselor.

We can do all things through Christ Jesus, but can do nothing without Him. We need Him for the healing of the soul and body.

We want to surrender to His delight and His desires for us. This, in turn, enables us to remain confident in being led by the Spirit in what He wants us to do.

We want to relinquish diet laws of "don't touch this" and "don't taste that" (Colossians 2:21) that dull our senses, and rather focus on turning our gazes on Jesus. Diet laws are what man established to institute an answer *outside* of Christ, trying to help a lost and fallen world of people—people who are wandering around not knowing how to do life, because they are outside the Spirit's leadership.

We want to come to His table of feasting and to dine with Him for fellowship, intimacy, wisdom, and direction.

We have the privilege of sitting at the table the Lord has made for us before our enemies of emotional eating, binge eating, disordered eating, and false identity in the soul and body, and to, once and for all, discover freedom. Are we ready to get back to the truths God has for us?

Setting our minds above

Setting our minds on Christ means seeking His kingdom first, instead of meditating on the natural cares of this world.

It means repositioning our hearts away from worrying about what we shall eat, drink, or wear, and instead truly delighting in the Lord. It means witnessing and knitting our hearts together with His desires, and removing everything that comes into direct competition with our inner man's design, one that craves to be directed by Christ alone.

What is your treasure?

> Jesus said: For where your treasure is, there your heart will also be.
> — Matthew 6:21 NKJV

What are our eyes focusing on? Where is our gaze? On others? On our reflections in the mirror? On saying we want to glorify God in our bodies, His temple, but rather choosing to find answers outside of Him?

We mustn't let the enemy deceive us. God alone is the answer and we want to train our souls in Christ as the author and finisher of our faith. As we focus on Him and behold the light of His countenance, we allow His radiance to flow through to our hearts, souls, minds, and bodies. We want to focus on the simplicity that is in Christ (2 Corinthians 11:3).

> For it is the God who commanded light to shine out of darkness, who has shone in our hearts to give the light of the

knowledge of the glory of God in the face of Jesus Christ. But
we have this treasure in earthen vessels, that the excellence of
the power may be of God and not of us.
— 2 Corinthians 4:6–7 NKJV

The Word of God and Jesus the living Word become our
treasure as all we need is found in them.

What is the definition of treasure?

Our treasure is whatever we are storing up; what thoughts,
meditations, and desires do we have stored up in our minds?

The Greek word for treasure is *thēsaurós*. This is also the
Greek word for what we in English call a thesaurus. It holds
an abundance of words that help us conceptualize the truths
of many words.

That their hearts may be encouraged, being knit together in
love, and attaining to all riches of the full assurance of
understanding, to the knowledge of the mystery of God, both
of the Father and of Christ, in whom are hidden all the
treasures of wisdom and knowledge. Now this I say lest
anyone should deceive you with persuasive words.
— Colossians 2:2–4 NKJV

This treasure we should be holding on to in our hearts and
minds is the power of salvation and its ability to rescue,
restore, and heal. Unfortunately, sometimes we forget the
saving power of the cross for the healing of our souls, and
focus on just our earthen vessels.

Our focus and treasure should be the excellencies and power of God in us, not ourselves! Let our treasure be the promises of God, His kingdom, and His power in us, in order to see full and total health transformation.

The power of the eyes

> The eye is the lamp of the body. If your eyes are good, your
> whole body will be full of light.
> — Matthew 6:22 NKJV

Whatever we allow into our eyes will affect our bodies. For some reason, we are in a society that believes how we treat our bodies will let us see, hear, and focus on God more—for instance, "I can finally put all my attention on the things of God once I lose weight."

We, however, must choose to set our minds on things above. God already made all the sacrifices; we do not need to make any others, other than to lay down our lives for Him. This is our reasonable duty; however, many of us are creating unreasonable duties that are not necessary.

> But if your eyes are bad, your whole body will be full of
> darkness. If then the light within you is darkness, how great
> is that darkness!
> — Matthew 6:23 NKJV

Sadly, this is the truth. If our eyes are bad, if our focus and our gaze are corrupt, this will *affect our bodies*—even if the light of Christ is within us, but we still only focus on darkness. The darkness is the negatives, the problems, the cares, and the stresses of life. This should be a huge wake-up call to us to change our focus.

> No one can serve two masters; for either he will hate the one and love the other, or he will stand by and be devoted to the one and despise and be against the other. You cannot serve God and mammon (deceitful riches, money, possessions, or whatever is trusted in).
> — Matthew 6:24 AMPC

We cannot serve God and then try to serve another god in our lives. It is impossible, and it's time to wake up. Do we despise God's leading in us when we want to do something else, another plan, another program, idolizing the body?

What have we been devoting our time, money, and affections to in the name of gaining health, body size, or freedom from food idols?

> Therefore I tell you, stop being perpetually uneasy (anxious and worried) about your life, what you shall eat or what you shall drink; or about your body, what you shall put on. Is not life greater [in quality] than food, and the body [far above and more excellent] than clothing?
> — Matthew 6:25 AMPC

Matthew 6:25 teaches us that the root is anxiety, and that great distractions arise when we become perpetually uneasy, anxious, and worried about what we put in and on our bodies. The great news is that our Father knows what we need. Let's turn to Him!

> For the Gentiles (heathen) wish for and crave and diligently
> seek all these things, and your heavenly Father knows well
> that you need them all.
> — Matthew 6:32 AMPC

Let us refrain from seeking, craving, and wishing for the things the world meditates on. Let's together walk out of Egypt, with its old ways and plans, and rediscover that this is much easier with Christ. We will find freedom, not just for ourselves, but also for those around us. Beloved, it is time.

My mission here is to lift the lid and expose the works of the enemy, to break off the chains of deception. To set captives free, and to declare to us that freedom was purchased and provided for us over 2000 years ago.

This is not a diet; this is true and lasting freedom in Christ.

Recap and reflect

- Spirit-Full Eating is a journey of divine health through feasting on the Word and drawing from the Spirit to delight in the Lord and prosper in our souls. Review the definition of Spirit-Full Eating in this chapter and ask the Lord what this means for you.

- We trust the leadership of the Holy Spirit as we navigate our health decisions—all while walking in the Spirit and the fear of the Lord, our most extraordinary accountability partner. Who have been your accountability partners before now? What does it feel like to have the master strategist, the Holy Spirit and the fear of the Lord, as your accountability partner?

- We are learning how to navigate life and health with Christ and how not to conform to this world and its prescription for freedom.

- We choose to set our minds on Christ above, and to seek the kingdom of God primarily from within our hearts— first inside and then out, through to our souls and bodies.

- We come to His table of feasting, and dine with Him for fellowship, intimacy, wisdom, direction, and freedom. We are moving from disordered eating to learning His prescription for health.

- Our words, thoughts, and meditations have power. What is stored up in you? What have you been meditating on about your health, how to obtain health, and how you view your body? Be honest and write down everything that comes to mind.

- All the treasures of wisdom and knowledge we need for this journey are found in the Father and Christ alone. Paul charges us to not only recognize this, but also to not be deceived by other persuasive words. Have you been persuaded by plans, programs, and worldly wisdom outside of Christ? Journal these before the Lord.

Chapter 4
The Struggle

Scripture references

Luke 8:15; John 6:38–40

The false attempts

One of the things that I have been discovering as I survey my own and countless others' journeys of chasing weight loss, health, and food freedom is that something's not quite right. The confusion, the ups and downs, the worries, effort, and striving show something is amiss.

We have spent countless years, hours, and much money attempting to gain health or lose weight. We've tried! No one could say that we haven't worked hard or that we haven't put our all into this process. So many of us have given more than we have been pleased with in the name of "health." So why isn't it working?

We have been told that it's a lot to do with *willpower*!

"We need more willpower. That's what we need."

"We need another program, you know, *the* program that will be a game changer, once and for all."

And then we come across another program. "Oh, this program looks good; it must be the final answer."

Or, "Let me go back to a previous program that seemed to work."

Or how about, "I just need to get my emotions in check? If I can do that, then I've got it all together."

These meditations of the heart, however, will not fix the issue. This is a spiritual issue, and we can't fix a spiritual issue with just more willpower or another program.

> For I have come down from heaven, not to do My own will,
> but the will of Him who sent Me.
> — John 6:38 NKJV

Before we move on, a word of caution is necessary. We could even make Spirit-Full Eating another diet or program. This is why this journey should first be an inside work of the heart, soul, and mind.

Each of us is on an individual journey and, depending on the condition of the soil in our hearts and whether the correct seeds of truth were sown, many factors will determine if and when the seeds of truth grow into all they are meant to and bear fruit in our lives (Luke 8:15).

Why the struggle?

I want to share with you a revelation the Lord led me to. Through much research and study of how the mind works regarding the restriction of foods and the effects this has on the body, I found that restriction creates a rebound effect that causes us to go into excess, the opposite of temperance. (See the additional information section for further reading.)

I have witnessed and experienced this backlash, and many scientists have proven that when you restrict foods, after a while there is a boomerang effect of loss of control.

And what I've found with people who struggle with binge eating or overeating (and I was one of them) is that there is always a point where we can identify that somewhere in our journey we have believed a lie.

Let's use the thought processes behind restricting ice cream as an example:

"I mustn't have ice cream."

"I mustn't touch ice cream."

"I mustn't even have ice cream in the house."

"Why am I obsessed with thinking about ice cream?"

"I must stop thinking about ice cream."

"Okay, maybe just a little ice cream."

Then, when their willpower caves in and they start to eat ice cream, they suddenly say, "I'm not going to have just the one bowl of ice cream." They'll perhaps have three bowls of ice cream. Or, if they do have just one, it's riddled with guilt, shame, and condemnation—and so the cycle starts again.

Why? Because, again, trying to remedy an issue without first tackling the heart, soul, and mind will have short-lived results. Focusing on the problem draws more attention to the short-term solutions, and these distract us from this central point: Without a developed and healed soul, we cannot see long-term health and prosperity.

We want to see this in the Word; we don't want to lean on what we've seen with our natural eyes. We want to see this through the Word because we always want to stay rooted and grounded in Scripture.

The Lord was faithful to me in this, and what I share with you over the next few chapters radically changed my view and my life.

Recap and reflect

- Whether it is food, weight, or simply overcoming a health crisis, we are told we just need more willpower to overcome. However, John 6:38 speaks of not our will but God's. We want to have the same approach in every area of life. Can you identify where the lines between your will versus Christ's will have become blurred?

- In this chapter we recognize that there is often a rebound effect after we restrict. Starting "great" on Monday can get us into chaos by the weekend. Why do you think this is?

Chapter 5
Wait! This Has Been Going On from the Beginning?

Scripture references

1 Timothy 4:1–5; Genesis 2:8–9, 16–17; Genesis 3:1–6

The enemy, time and time again, from the beginning in Genesis onward, has tried to distort our view of God and our view of food.

The Bible very clearly says that it's through the doctrines of devils, the philosophies of men, and deceiving spirits that we are tricked into believing specific lies about food, marriage, life, and just about everything.

> Now the Spirit expressly says that in latter times some will depart from the faith, giving heed to deceiving spirits and doctrines of demons, speaking lies in hypocrisy, having their own conscience seared with a hot iron, forbidding to marry, and commanding to abstain from foods which God created to be received with thanksgiving by those who believe and know the truth. For every creature of God is good, and nothing is to be refused if it is received with thanksgiving; for it is sanctified by the word of God and prayer.
> — 1 Timothy 4:1–5 NKJV

Many food restrictions that we experience today stem from a second-century Gnostic teaching that the spirit is good and matter is evil. Paul worked diligently at the time to fight these lies.

Gnostics held the view that we need to abstain from pleasures in life because they distract us from God, and this often strong-held view was applied to food, money, and sex.

Money is a great tool for the kingdom, enabling us to provide for our families; however, the unnatural love for money is evil.

Sex within the covenant of marriage is a gift from God, but taken out of context it can be destructive.

Likewise, food itself is not evil—it is a gift from God when received with thanksgiving, the Word of God, and prayer.

It is, however, the abuse of food that leads one down a destructive path; the wrong view of food and the wrong view of our identity create havoc. And these issues with foods started much earlier—from the beginning, in Genesis.

Every tree pleasant to sight and good for food

Let's slowly go over these verses from Genesis so that we can catch what's going on.

> The Lord God planted a garden eastward in Eden, and there He put the man whom He had formed. And out of the ground the Lord God made every tree grow that is pleasant to the sight and good for food. The tree of life was also in the midst

of the garden, and the tree of the knowledge of good and evil.
— Genesis 2:8–9 NKJV

Let's pause there for a minute. God said that every tree that came out of the ground He created to be pleasant to the sight and good for food, and in Genesis 1:31 God says that everything He made is good.

This would include both the tree of life and the tree of the knowledge of good and evil—one of the other trees created for pleasant sight and good for food that was also in the middle of the garden.

Of every tree you may freely eat

So now, let's carefully read what God says.

> And the Lord God commanded the man, saying, "Of every tree of the garden you may freely eat."
> — Genesis 2:16 NKJV.

Not only did God command that of every tree we may freely eat, but He began with the freedom and good news first—before moving on to verse 17 with the parameters.

> But of the tree of the knowledge of good and evil you shall not eat, for in the day that you eat of it you shall surely die.
> — Genesis 2:17 NKJV

Now let's look at what the serpent said about what God said.

> Now the serpent was more cunning than any beast of the field
> which the Lord God had made. And he said to the woman,
> "Has God indeed said, 'You shall not eat of every tree of the
> garden'?"
> — Genesis 3:1 NKJV

Now, often we just skip along, but I want you to pay close
attention for a minute to what God actually said.

God said in Genesis 2:16, "Of every tree of the garden, you
may freely eat."

But Satan implies that God said, "You shall not eat of every
tree of the garden."

Let's now look at what Eve said.

> And the woman said to the serpent, "We may eat the fruit of
> the trees of the garden; but of the fruit of the tree which is in
> the midst of the garden, God has said, 'You shall not eat it, nor
> shall you touch it, lest you die.'"
> — Genesis 3:2–3 NKJV

Notice here that Eve added that God said she mustn't even
touch the fruit of the tree of the knowledge of good and evil.

The beguile of Satan

> Then the serpent said to the woman, "You will not surely die.
> For God knows that in the day you eat of it your eyes will be
> opened, and you will be like God, knowing good and evil." So
> when the woman saw that the tree was good for food, that it
> was pleasant to the eyes, and a tree desirable to make one
> wise, she took of its fruit and ate. She also gave to her

husband with her, and he ate.
— Genesis 3:4–6 NKJV

So let us recap and look at the three ways the instructions were given.

- God said the truth. In Genesis 2:16 He said, "Of every tree of the garden, you may freely eat."

- Then, in Genesis 3:1, Satan had his interpretation and lied about what God said. Satan implied that God said, "You shall not eat of every tree."

- And then Eve also had her misinterpretation of what God said. Framing it as, "God has said, 'You shall not eat it, nor shall you touch it, lest you die.'" (Genesis 3:3).

Comparison of the versions of the instruction

God	Of every tree of the garden you may freely eat but of the tree of the knowledge of good and evil, you shall not eat ...
The serpent	You shall not eat of every tree?
Eve	You shall not eat it, nor touch it, lest you die.

And there is such a subtle shift. The question that Satan asked Eve in turn made her change what God had said, because God didn't say they shouldn't touch it.

He clearly didn't say don't touch it. And He also said you may freely eat, except for the one tree. Satan turned it into "You shall not eat of every tree." Eve then said, "No, no, God said we can, but not this one."

Why am I focusing on this point? Well, first of all, I never saw that subtle difference between what God said and what Satan brought into his question to Eve.

I never actually saw that initial shift, but it's important because what usually happens when Satan brings in conflicting information is that it is very subtle.

The Bible states he was the most cunning and sneakiest of all, so he brought in this shift in phrase to get Eve to question and reinterpret something different from what God had said.

When the Lord brought this to my attention, I think I was up at 3:30 in the morning. I was on the floor in my office, just crying because I'd never realized how the tricks started with Eve. We all know she was deceived, but deceived in such a way? So subtle, but with such great implications for humankind.

I too have experienced and witnessed how the world and the prince of this air have caused us to question the truth about food, about what God has for us. God says all food is a gift from Him. We, however, live in a society that has made us look at food as the enemy, as a torment. Or to think that we have a God who withholds good things.

Recap and reflect

- In this chapter we saw how the enemy deceived Eve by twisting words the Father had given her and Adam. Through questioning and doubt, Eve lost track of who she was and of what God had already given them.

- In 1 Timothy 4:1–2 Paul states that in the latter days many will be deceived in the same way by deceiving spirits and the doctrines of devils. This is because their consciences have been dulled or seared to the unction of the Holy Spirit. Our goal is to again become sensitive to the guidance of the Lord, so that we can walk in His footsteps.

- Since, in this chapter, we have gone back to the beginning, let's go back to your beginning, or maybe even to some views you still hold. Consider your history with food. List all your beliefs about food, or health, or about how God sees you because of what you have been told or taught. For example, some of the ones I've heard are: eggs are "bad," then they are "good" again; bread is literally the devil, stay away from it; or don't eat after 7 p.m. Next, take some time in prayer and just give these over to the Lord. Entrust your heart and all you have learned to Him.

- Reflect on the verses shared from Genesis.

Prayer

Thank You, Lord, for being my firm foundation. You are my cornerstone. You don't change with the seasons. You don't move with the times of the age. You don't shift like the other kingdoms. Thank You for building and guarding my body! In Jesus' name. Amen.

Chapter 6
The Master Distracter

Scripture references

Galatians 5:13, 5:1; James 1:5; Romans 12:2, Isaiah 11:1–3

So, why does Satan try to trick humankind in the way discussed in the previous chapter? I believe it's primarily to tarnish the character of God, and also to tarnish how the church is viewed.

When I became a Christian, I expected the church to be the healthiest group of people on the planet because they've got God living inside them. However, I saw how many are still struggling in the area of health—they're broken and battling with what to do and how. I believe that Satan's ultimate plan is to distract us from fulfilling the Great Commission and from what God has called us to do.

If he can get us focused on all these worries and cares about what to eat and drink, and all the things that are going wrong, and all the ways the world says to fix them, it is a huge distraction—a huge, huge distraction from the Great Commission.

I'm not saying that, now, because we are going to walk in freedom, it doesn't matter how we care for our bodies, and so cast off honoring the temple. To do so would violate scripture.

> For you, brethren, have been called to liberty; only do not use liberty as an opportunity for the flesh, but through love serve one another.
> — Galatians 5:13 NKJV

But rather, what we are meant to do with this freedom is to serve one another in love—this is what God is saying. And then:

> Stand fast therefore in the liberty wherewith Christ hath made us free, and be not entangled again with the yoke of bondage.
> — Galatians 5:1 KJV

A cover up?

In today's culture we see that the obsession with the way we look and treat the body, together with the overconsumption of food, can also try to falsely cover the holes that are in our souls—holes that only Christ can fill.

No matter how we have replaced Christ, whether by turning to food for comfort, or by obsessing over losing weight in order to feel confident, we no longer see our need for Him. Why would we need the fullness of Christ if we can get all of this ourselves through false comforts, vices, and natural means in our own strength?

So, just like with Eve, Satan wants us to believe that God is stingy and that He withholds good things. If we hold this same view, we will be tempted to rebel, just as Eve did.

As I previously said, restriction has been proven to cause a rebound effect. I believe that the enemy will use gluttony, and he'll use athleticism or restriction. I don't think he really cares either way. His goal is to get us to turn our gazes away from the fullness God has for us. The enemy wants us to believe that God was a withholder in the garden, and that He's still a withholder now.

If somebody is operating in gluttony, then this is turning their attention away from God. If they enforce restrictions, then this too is distracting them from the Lord. Either way, the enemy accomplishes his purpose. Right? Either way, whichever way you look at it, his purpose is being achieved.

Come to Me for wisdom

God wants us to care for and tend to the temple that is our body. The Bible speaks about how the body belongs to Holy Spirit.

> Don't you realize that your body is the temple of the Holy Spirit, who lives in you and was given to you by God? You do not belong to yourself.
> — 1 Corinthians 6:19 NLT

Both David and Solomon were directed by God and instructed as to how to build and care for the temple of God, which they called God's house. Can you imagine if David and Solomon had received this mandate and then decided to ask the Philistines how to build and maintain the house of the Lord? Seeking ungodly counsel goes against Psalm 1:1 and is forbidden by God.

There are millions of believers around the world, whose bodies are temples of the Holy Spirit, who are seeking the counsel of the ungodly pertaining to the health and wellbeing of their bodies. And this when it is God Himself who has designed the body and made the laws that govern its benefit.

> Therefore, "Come out from among them
> And be separate," says the Lord.
> — 2 Corinthians 6:17 NKJV

Let us draw near to the manufacturer and master designer of our bodies, souls, minds, and spirits.

James 1:5 thankfully tells us what to do if any of us lacks wisdom. He is the One we should seek!

> If any of you lacks wisdom [to guide him through a decision or circumstance], he is to ask of [our benevolent] God, who gives to everyone generously and without rebuke or blame, and it will be given to him.
> — James 1:5 AMP

You may be saying, "I don't even fully understand the depths of this." Pause, ask God to allow this to really touch your heart so that you can see what God is saying.

I believe that God wanted to teach Adam and Eve to walk in wisdom, knowledge, and revelation—after all, we have been created in His image. But to do so from within relationship with Him, not outside of it. And not by eating of the tree of knowledge of good and evil outside of God. He said not to do that.

The reason we know God wants us to have knowledge, revelation, and wisdom is because Romans 12:2 says that we are to renew our minds so we'll be able to discern between good and evil. But also, He's given us His Spirit. The Holy Spirit is the Spirit of wisdom, revelation, and knowledge. So, it's not that He doesn't want us to have knowledge and wisdom about life, but it has to come through Him, through relationship.

The enemy will always attempt to pervert truth and distract us with counterfeits. However, we have a master strategist living on the inside of us—the Holy Spirit—and He will direct us into truth, wisdom, and knowledge.

> Out of the stump of David's family will grow a shoot— yes, a new Branch bearing fruit from the old root. **And the Spirit of the Lord will rest on him— the Spirit of wisdom and understanding, the Spirit of counsel and might, the Spirit of knowledge and the fear of the Lord**. He will delight in

obeying the Lord. He will not judge by appearance nor make a decision based on hear-say.
— Isaiah 11:1–3 NLT (emphasis added)

The Great Commission

After His resurrection, Jesus gave His disciples a most important instruction before His ascension into heaven.

> Then the eleven disciples went away into Galilee, to the mountain which Jesus had appointed for them. When they saw Him, they worshipped Him; but some doubted. And Jesus came and spoke to them, saying, "All authority has been given to Me in heaven and on earth. Go therefore and make disciples of all the nations, baptizing them in the name of the Father and of the Son and of the Holy Spirit, teaching them to observe all things that I have commanded you; and lo, I am with you always, even to the end of the age."
> — Matthew 28:16–20 NKJV

With the distractions of emphasis on eating and drinking, and focus on body size, and all that comes with them, we ultimately take our eyes off fulfilling the Great Commission. We are distracted, so we hold back on God's full agenda for our lives in Christ.

A testimony

(Names and places changed for privacy.)

I was raised as Catholic before I accepted Christ into my life when I was in my early twenties, and so I didn't know about missionaries, or anything like that, and I was so excited about the Great Commission. I wanted to share so much with the world how much God loved me.

And so, I went on staff with a Christian organization and had to raise financial support. I was going to go to Swaziland to teach there, and to use that as a platform to share the Gospel, to disciple students, and to do discipleship in the community.

During the preparation process, I went on a very extreme and restrictive diet. And I weighed very little for my height. During this process, God raised all my financial support within weeks and this reinforced the belief that this is what He wanted, that this was His will for my life.

Then I started eating more food, and within one week of eating this way, I had gained twelve pounds. And so that continued and I ended up regaining quickly. While I went through training (it was four months of intense Bible training) I gained all of the weight back, plus more. I was more than double my original size.

And so, as a result, this Christian organization (this was in the early seventies, a long time ago, and they've changed since then) put me on a standard of performance that restricted my eating. I had two choices each day of how many calories I could eat, depending on how much I exercised, and if I ate healthy food. For each thing I didn't do each day, I had to pay five dollars. So it could be up to fifteen dollars a day.

I was a missionary at that time, making about a hundred dollars a month, so you know that was a lot of money to pay over. And it was a big deal. I didn't gain any weight, but I didn't lose weight either. But that in itself was kind of a miracle to me, that it stopped increasing.

Because I didn't make their targets, I was told they had decided that I was a carnal Christian. Because I didn't have my weight under control, they considered it insubordination, and said that I hadn't met the criteria for staying on staff.

So, I was terminated from staff and the head of this mission organization wanted me to write a letter to my supporters, explaining all that to them. So, the failure I experienced, the shame, the guilt—I cannot begin to tell you what that was like. It was so public. I had to confess it all to all these people who had invested in me to go and do God's work, and then it just fit into my insecurities.

I believed the lie that I couldn't even serve God because I was such a sinful carnal Christian. I ended up going through years of feeling like a complete failure in my life because I believed I was so sinful.

Fortunately, God led me to a minister, and he really helped me tremendously with dealing with this trauma, but it was still there. When it haunts me, that guilt and shame, and feeling like a failure, I have to always go back to God's Word. Everything Sophia is teaching, I felt like was lived out exactly in my own life and Satan temporarily won in terms of this. I didn't get to go and serve the Lord then as I could have.

That's no longer the case. I eventually did continue to do ministry on my own and ended up going to teach in Kenya. I started a program for kids with special needs there. So, God did answer that desire in my life. I continue to work in the mission field today.

There is hope

Such a powerful testimony. We see the enemy will even creep into the church to distort truth and, in this case, base someone's ability to serve on their size and their eating habits.

I understand why the world struggles, but why does the church? I think it's because the enemy knows that we are the light and the salt of the earth. If he can keep us dampened, if he can keep us distracted, then he has won.

We recognize there's a problem, and there's a worldly, carnal tool to try to fix it. It's the great bait-and-switch tactic because he doesn't want us to know it's him. He wants us to think it's us.

And again, it's that same blame and condemnation that gets us to think like that. Even now, when reading this, many will say, "Well, it's not all the enemy. I am guilty too." They may hear the voice of condemnation and guilt as they read this.

God is not disappointed with any of us because, again, we're judging when we think God is disappointed. What we're saying is that God is looking at us according to our flesh but, in contrast, Jeremiah 31:34 says He chooses not to remember the sins He has forgiven us for. When God looks at us, He looks at us from our spirits and through what Christ has done.

And so, when the voice of the accuser (sadly sometimes even in the church) tells us that God is disappointed with us because of our size, it is a lie. Then, if you have guilt and condemnation, you can't do anything. You can't function with guilt and condemnation because it grips and holds you down.

Recap and reflect

- The enemy is a master distracter, tempting us to heavily focus on the problem, and not on Christ, and not on the Great Commission. What have you been holding back from doing due to the distraction? Ask the Holy Spirit where you may have been deceived.

- Although we have been called to freedom, we are not called to use this as an opportunity for the flesh. We use our freedom to glorify God and serve others. How has Christ called you? What has been holding you back?

- The enemy will use obsession, compulsiveness, asceticism, gluttony, or restriction—he is not partial to which one. Each one serves the same purpose. Have you faced struggles with all or some of these?

- We do not want to go the Philistines or the world for direction on how to look after the temple of God. Spend some time asking God for *His* insights on how wonderfully He has made your body, His temple.

- We seek God for counsel and wisdom (James 1:5) because here we find safety. Are you ready to pivot at any moment when the Lord leads?

Prayer

Lord, we repent of heeding distractions all the times we have allowed ourselves to be moved. Forgive us for being distracted by the temporary and changing wisdom of this age.

You only did what the Father showed you. We want to be more like You, Jesus. Help us to focus and take authority over every assignment from the enemy to distract us from the Great Commission and Your mission for our lives.

We renounce confusion, and we stand focused on Your heart, Your way, and Your truth. We come against every spirit that tries to mislead us and divert our attention from keeping our minds on You.

We need wisdom and insight from heaven, so we seek you diligently. In Jesus' name. Amen.

Chapter 7
The Spirit Expressly Says

Scripture references

1 Timothy 4; John 8:44; Colossians 2; Matthew 22:36–39; 1 John 3:23

Previously we looked at 1 Timothy chapter 4, where the Holy Spirit speaks to Paul as he is writing to Timothy. Paul opens verse 1 by saying, "Now the Spirit expressly says." We can see that "expressly" here is a powerful word. The Amplified Bible states, "But the [Holy] Spirit explicitly and unmistakably declares..."

We must, therefore, pay attention with earnest hearts, as He expects us to be fully aware of what's happening.

> Now the Spirit expressly says that in latter times some will depart from the faith, giving heed to deceiving spirits and doctrines of demons.
> — 1 Timothy 4:1 NKJV

Paul says that in the latter times some will depart from the faith and, when studying that passage of scripture, I always thought it means to lose faith in Christ, to deny Christ; that's not what it solely means. It also means not putting our complete trust and confidence in Him, not having complete dependence on and trust in God and His ways entirely.

Some people are going to depart from that by giving heed to deceiving spirits and the doctrines of devils. So, what are these deceiving spirits and doctrines of devils?

These are the teachings, philosophies, and opinions built on lies from the father of lies. We can be gripped by these opinions rather than by the voice of God.

Giving heed

What does "giving heed" mean? It means to
- give attention to something
- attach yourself, to devote thought and effort to something (Thayer's Greek English Lexicon)
- hold the mind (Strong's Concordance)

When we meditate long enough on a lie, we begin to believe it and to act on it. The lies I had believed about food, health, and my body became my reference point, and it took many years to unravel them.

What can happen is that our consciences—the ability to know right from wrong—become tainted. Then we are no longer convicted that what we are doing doesn't please God, or that it is not good for our souls or body.

For example, when I was in a weight loss class and desperate to lose weight, I would take laxative products, just so the scale would show a smaller number. Today I look back at that in shock! However, back in those days, it seemed utterly normal to me. Over time, and through repeatedly doing so, I progressively became desensitized to the voice of the Lord in the area of health. It took a wake-up call from the Spirit to jolt me out of this disordered pattern.

I have often counseled others who state that they can hear God in other areas of life, but struggle to hear Him when it relates to their health. This can indeed be confusing for many. I have seen that this can happen if we repeatedly brush off the unction of the Lord—it's then less likely we will be sensitive to His voice.

The good news is we can guard our consciences by keeping free from the hypocrisies and lies of these last days.

Satan was trying to trick Eve from the beginning in the garden by saying, and I paraphrase, "God is quite restrictive here. He doesn't want you to eat freely from the trees. Are you sure? That's not what He said!" This matches Satan's character and nature; he is a liar and deceives many.

> He was a murderer from the beginning. He has always hated the truth because there is no truth in him. When he lies, it is consistent with his character; for he is a liar and the Father of lies.
> — John 8:44 NLT

Satan doesn't care whether it's bingeing, gluttony, or heavy restrictions; he will use any method. He wants us to believe God is a withholder of good things. Many people eat in excess or binge because they have fallen into Satan's trap—he knows that even the mere idea of potential restriction can cause someone to obsess over a particular food. Eve was happy to ignore the fruit God had previously mentioned not to eat, until it was brought to her attention as a restriction.

It is these same deceiving evil spirits that lie to us today; Paul continues:

> forbidding to marry, and commanding to abstain from foods which God created to be received with thanksgiving by those who believe and know the truth. For every creature of God is good, and nothing is to be refused if it is received with thanksgiving; for it is sanctified by the word of God and prayer.
> — 1 Timothy 4:3–4 NKJV

With Spirit-Full Eating, we recognize that there are many lies and doctrines we have been led to believe about food and health. We are tearing down these lies and returning to knowing that God is good. He gives good gifts, like food, which we will receive with the power of thanksgiving, the Word of God, and prayer.

In 1 Timothy 4:1 Paul says anyone who teaches these lies originates from the enemy. There is a concerted effort by many to teach that certain foods are wrong and that we should abstain from them. Now that we know the origins of these lies, we have to acknowledge that anyone commanding us to abstain from specific foods is under the influence of the doctrine of evil spirits.

We don't fight against flesh and blood. In fact, Paul didn't say it is individuals. He said it's the deceiving spirits and doctrines of demons. And we know that in the garden Satan, the master of all the demons, was the one who tricked Eve.

I am not saying that if God led you not to eat something for a season that this is an evil spirit you are hearing. However, anything or anyone demanding that you follow specific food rules, or do not touch, or do not taste, is problematic. (Please read the disclaimer in the additional information section of the book.) Also, if it's seen that eating a particular food is the right thing to do and those who do the opposite are wrong, then this, too, is not from the Lord. Everything we need is fulfilled in Christ.

> Let no one cheat you of your reward, taking delight in false humility and worship of angels, intruding into those things which he has not seen, vainly puffed up by his fleshly mind, and not holding fast to the Head, from whom all the body, nourished and knit together by joints and ligaments, grows with the increase that is from God. Therefore, if you died with Christ from the basic principles of the world, why, as though living in the world, do you subject yourselves to regulations— "Do not touch, do not taste, do not handle," which all concern things which perish with the using—according to the commandments and doctrines of men? These things indeed have an appearance of wisdom in self-imposed religion, false

humility, and neglect of the body, but are of no value against
the indulgence of the flesh.
— Colossians 2:18–23 NKJV

Often, we are engaged in extreme restrictions to puff
ourselves up. We think we are somehow better than another
for eating a particular food, like a salad. Have you experienced
that? Are we being "good" if we choose the salad with no
dressing, and "bad" if we have a slice of cheesecake? Are we
an "angel" for eating only no- or low-carb foods, but sinning
if we eat a sandwich? In fact, some diet programs even call
certain foods "syns" as a play on words, implying "sins."

There are no scriptures that detail specific foods as either
good or bad under the New Covenant, and we would do best
to avoid adding points of view that are not in the Bible.

Paul says (in Colossians 2:16–23, 3:11) that by elevating
practices of denial or rituals of eating we are losing the truth
that Christ is all and is in all, when He is what we need. We
need Christ to take the first place in our lives as our head.

Walking with Christ prioritizes relationship over
legalism, that is, don't touch this or eat that. Our primary
focus is to get back to allowing the leadership of the Spirit,
and for our hearts, souls, and bodies to follow where He leads.

We also see this when Jesus was tempted in the desert.
What was the first temptation He experienced there?
Matthew 4:3 tells us that after fasting for forty days and forty

nights, Jesus was hungry. The tempter came to Him and said, "If you are the Son of God, tell these stones to become bread." But Jesus answered, "It is written that man shall not live on bread alone, but on every word that comes from the mouth of God." Jesus prioritized relationship with His Father.

Our goal is evident! If we are meant to focus on something other than the rules and regulations surrounding foods, what should we do? Are we fed up with the conflicting and hypocritical advice in today's modern society, and do we feel at a loss? Let's go to the head that is Christ and hear what He has to say.

> "Teacher, which is the most important commandment in the law of Moses?" Jesus replied, "'You must love the Lord your God with all your heart, all your soul, and all your mind.' This is the first and greatest commandment. A second is equally important: 'Love your neighbor as yourself.'"
> — Matthew 22:36–39 NLT

> And this is his commandment: We must believe in the name of his Son, Jesus Christ, and love one another, just as he commanded us.
> — 1 John 3:23 NLT

Loving God and walking in relationship with Him will cause us to do the right thing by treating our body, His body, the correct way. And, in turn, how we love others will change as we will now have more freedom to love and serve. We have spent far too long living from the outside in. Through relationship with Him, the Holy Spirit will categorically lead us into what is suitable for our health, life, souls, and bodies.

Recap and reflect

- "Departing from faith" can mean not trusting God fully in His plan and answer for us. This is a sign of the latter times we are living in. Have you made Jesus the Lord of your health?

- We have been giving heed to the principles of this world for health; giving heed, by definition, includes giving attention to, and devoting ourselves to in thought and deed. What voices have you been giving heed to?

- When we believe lies, over time they can cause our consciences in a specific area to be seared or dulled. This can limit our hearing from the Lord regarding our health. Repent today of not listening to the voice of the Lord over your health, and apply the blood of Jesus to wash your conscience (Hebrews 9:14).

- Our mission is to focus on Christ, to develop intimacy, to remove the lies, and to receive healing in our hearts. Recommit to the Lord today.

- Let us change our thinking that foods are morally good or bad, and that eating them determines our worth, or is the sole answer for our health.

Prayer

Dear Lord, You are sovereign over my health; I repent of believing the lies of the enemy by taking heed to the thoughts and opinions of this world.

Lord, open my eyes to see if I've been battling something that I thought was of myself, but is actually energized by forces that are often unseen but very real.

I trust You on this journey of healing for my soul. Lord, when You lead me to do something, I will do it, and I believe You will protect me.

I declare that I do not live by bread alone; I declare that I will live and not die, and I declare the wonderful deeds of the Lord!

Thank you, Lord, for your protection over me. In Jesus' name. Amen.

Chapter 8
The Abundance

Scripture reference

Zechariah 4:6-7

We have seen how, from Genesis to Matthew, and from Colossians to Timothy, there is a plan of the enemy to try to trick us into either restricting food or obsessing over it. He tempts us with food and wants us to have the wrong viewpoint, to see food as other than being an amazing gift from God. The enemy's ultimate aim is to get us to believe that we serve a very restrictive God who withholds good things from us. The enemy is always trying to distort the gifts of God. Ultimately, if he can distract us, our souls cannot prosper and effectively do the will of God.

One of the things I noticed in Genesis is that God started by telling Adam and Eve: These are all the wonderful foods you can eat. The Father didn't start by telling them about the one tree that shouldn't be eaten of. God started with and emphasized what was freely available to them.

I can imagine how, with this one tree surrounded by an abundance of fruit trees and vegetables, God put the focus on all of the beautiful things first. And next He said, "But just this one, just this one, I don't want you to eat from it." And similarly, the enemy tries to get us to not focus on all the wonderful things we can or should be eating, but rather on the minute details above and beyond the heart of God.

I was incredibly moved when God first showed me this, when I realized that this is indeed spiritual warfare. The world will tell us, "You have this battle with food; you need to cut this and that out." Or, "You need to lose 100 pounds, work hard, cut out x, and eat healthily." Outside of Christ this is simplistic and works driven.

> So he said to me, "This is the word of the LORD to Zerubbabel: Not by might nor by power, but by My Spirit, says the LORD of Hosts. What are you, O great mountain? Before Zerubbabel you will become a plain. Then he will bring forth the capstone accompanied by shouts of 'Grace, grace to it!'"
> — Zechariah 4:6–7 BSB

This battle is spiritual, and we can't fix a spiritual issue by natural means. It won't come by might or by our strength. Not in the beginning, the middle, or the end.

And even in my own life, I always knew there was a battle going on but, until I had this realization, I didn't fully understand the degree to which this is going on all around us. And it is one of the biggest deceptions of the enemy.

Where does our fullness come from?

Paul was very clever while writing under the leading of the Holy Spirit. The false teachers at the time were teaching that fullness and freedom come from abstaining from foods and pleasure (sound familiar?), but Paul taught that the fullness and freedom we desire come through Christ, and Christ alone. That's why Paul used words such as "fullness," "beholding," and "holding fast to the head that is Christ." Jesus died for us to know our true identities and the law of liberty. He has provided for us His way and His freedom.

Abstaining and having restrictive mindsets can, as previously said, create a rebound effect. This can lead to the overconsumption of food, or we may start to despise or abuse food. This can also include the abuse of the body. Think of people who have bulimia or anorexia, or those who over-exercise to the point where they're harming their bodies. They are despising the temple itself.

Once the enemy can get us to change the image of what the body looks like in our minds, we start to despise God's creation, our own bodies. Whether we see ourselves as of a larger size or look enviously at somebody who has lost a lot of weight, it's unhealthy either way.

We were made in the image of God. Satan's plan is to distort that image in our minds or bodies. We're taking back the image God has given us by recognizing the fullness that we already have within us!

We have the fullness of God radiating from within our spirits. It is an amazing truth, and our goal is for this to flow through our souls so that we can walk out the fullness of Christ in every area of our lives.

We want our hearts to so greatly overflow with this fullness of God that no other counterfeit vice can have a look-in—to be so filled with the joy of the Lord that is our strength.

Recap and reflect

- The enemy is trying to get us to distort our perception of food as an amazing gift from God. Our negative view of foods can prevent our souls from prospering and may cause many disordered eating patterns. Ask the Lord to search your heart for false beliefs and praise Him for His creation of your body.

- We can't battle this mountain in our own strength or might. When we focus on the fullness of God within us, it begins internally. As we behold Him, we will be changed.

- Our spirits are perfect in their identity in Christ. Our goal is to have this truth flow to all the parts of our souls for healing and true transformation. We will take back what the enemy has stolen. What are you ready to cast before the feet of Jesus in this journey?

Chapter 9
The Great Takeback

Scripture references

Luke 10:19; Matthew 19:26; John 8:32; Romans 12:2; 1 John 4:1; Hebrews 5:14

We know that God is to be loved and trusted, that we can treasure Him, that He's full of wisdom, and that He knows exactly what we need. Why then do so many of us struggle with the idea of being led by the Spirit? Often, because we've been deceived, our attempts have failed. As a result, we can build a habit of quitting, of giving up. But we can also choose to build a habit of surrendering to God and winning the war!

> Behold, I have given you authority to tread on serpents and scorpions and over all the enemy's power, and nothing shall hurt you.
> — Luke 10:19 ESV

We have built layer upon layer of wrong doctrines and misconceptions. These build strongholds in the mind, creating, in the long run, a platform for the enemy.

These strongholds have to be pulled down and smashed. We need to rebuild and bring in truth, flooding the gates of our souls with wisdom and knowledge that can only come from the Spirit of God.

As we let the glory of God come in, our bodies will be in health as our souls prosper. We will then take back what the enemy has stolen.

> But Jesus looked at them and said, "With people [as far as it depends on them], it is impossible, but with God all things are possible."
> — Matthew 19:26 AMP

With God all things are possible for those who believe.

My takeback

The Lord prompted me to analyze how I had been tricked into forming strongholds. I had experienced years of restriction, filled with a dieting mindset, the principles of man, and destructive habits.

God spoke to me about enjoying the foods He had made in order to help me break free from the chains that bound me. He wanted me to have and to live in freedom, and to focus on all the wonderful God-made foods that so many diets stated were "wrong" or "bad."

Like Eve, Satan tried to trick me and distort God's words. He used lies such as, "Did God really say that?" "Did He really say you can eat freely, or was He saying only eat the foods God made?" The subtle additional word "only" began to change the whole truth of what God was saying to me.

God was saying to eat freely, but the enemy subtly turned it around to make me believe that God was saying (in a harsh, condemning way) *only* to eat the foods He made, or else! It was easy to make me believe this lie because I had not yet fully believed that God was well able to heal me His way.

I had many strongholds that, through listening to the enemy's lies, I thought were my personal beliefs, and that it was God speaking. It's imperative on this journey to test every voice and every spirit (Romans 12:2; 1 John 4:1; Hebrews 5:14).

Satan has always planned to distort God's truth and His words. When the enemy is involved, it is indeed a war. This is not about, "Oh, I'm just a bad person, and I can never stick to anything."

This means we need to change the way we address life. When we recognize we're in a spiritual war, God has an answer for how to deal with spiritual warfare.

The enemy's goal is fourfold: distort, distract, deceive, and doubt. He wants to distort our views, distract us from the answer, deceive us with lies, and to cause us to doubt God and who we are in Him.

A lot of us do not even realize that this is spiritual. We may not be accountable for what we don't know, but we *are* accountable for the way that we handle this information we now have. It's what we do with it that's so important.

And you shall know the truth, and the truth shall make you free.
— John 8:32 NKJV

Recap and reflect

- We have been given authority in Christ, and we will overcome this battle!

- We are in a spiritual battle, and there is a fourfold approach of the enemy: to distort, to distract, to deceive, and to cause doubt.

- Have you been lied to? Has your thinking about food, your image, or even your identity been distorted?

- Knowing that the enemy can twist reality, what is God asking you to do?

- What have been the effects of the enemy's fourfold approach in your life?

Prayer

Heavenly Father, I glorify Your name today because You are the truth. I want to receive beauty for ashes. I acknowledge You as my Father, and I trust that You will help me and bring me into the whole truth. So, I rejoice in, rely on, trust, and praise Your holy name and You alone. You alone will do it, and I will follow Your lead. Hallelujah! In this fight, I say no more to guilt, shame, and condemnation for myself and for others.

Lord, open my eyes to finally realize that it actually has nothing to do with food. It's a spiritual battle. The moment that I gave my life to Christ, my spirit matched Christ's image. Satan hates Jesus, and so I recognize that when he sees me, he hates me too. He has therefore tried to trick me and to cunningly deceive me, as he did Eve.

Lord, I thank You that You're revealing the truth at this moment. I lay down my way of fighting. I choose to stand still and wait on You. I wage the good warfare by resting in Your finished work of the cross and by remaining in Your truth. I will not go to the left or to the right, no matter what is being said. I will stand firm in the whole armor of God, so that I will know how to fight and how to stand.

Lord, I silence the voice of the accuser and break every lie that has kept me bound or tricked me for years. Show me where I have used the carnal weapons of dieting, restriction, or overindulgence to deal with spiritual warfare and battle.

Using these carnal weapons is crippling the world, and killing off the next generation and the church. So, Lord, I pray for the church. I pray for the leaders. I pray, Lord God, that all women and men will find freedom, and will fulfill the Great Commission and calling on their lives.

I love You, and I thank You, in Jesus' name. Amen.

Chapter 10
The Fullness

Scripture references

Romans 15:13; Colossians 2:6–7; Luke 17:11–19; Isaiah 26:3; Matthew 12:35; John 17:10–11; Acts 13:52; 2 Corinthians 7:4; Ephesians 1:23, 3:19, 4:10

We want to focus on walking in the fullness of God. Let's look at the four keys to seeing the fullness of God flow through to our souls.

The imagination

This is setting our minds on the finished work of what God is doing in and through us. What does the finished work of healing look like for us? What does freedom look like for us? Hope is a confident expectation in our imaginations, set on the promises of God before us. We need to rehearse in our hearts the ways God has brought us through (Romans 15:13).

Giving thanks and glorifying God

We are to glorify God, and to value and prize Him above all — for everything He has done, is doing, and for who He is (Colossians 2:6–7). We can spend our entire lives giving thanks for this. We can also choose to take food and give thanks for how God has provided and made this for us, and for the hands that prepared it.

When Jesus healed the ten lepers in Luke 17:11–19 and only one returned to thank and praise Him, we are shown the importance of giving thanks to Jesus for His work. Thanksgiving and faith in Christ alone can bring healing. Through thanksgiving we can walk in humility. It causes us to give our cares to Him, takes our eyes off the problem, and puts our focus on the answer. We choose to magnify the promise over the problem (Isaiah 26:3).

A heart that desires to worship Him

Worship is not simply the songs we sing, but our lives laid down as living sacrifices. When we give our plans over to Him, it moves His heart. Let us take the time to surrender our plans. Let's journal any false lies we may have believed about how the Father sees our health or eating. Let's bring our souls into His presence today because there is the fullness of joy there.

A change of heart and conscience

Often, we look at the external issues and get into the busy work of behavior modification without prioritizing the condition of our hearts. It simply doesn't work. The heart and conscience can become desensitized and hardened during the years of trials and difficulties and working at healing in our own strength.

When this happens, we become less sensitive to the leading of the Holy Spirit in our spirits, and more sensitive to the dominance of the flesh. If we want to see changes in behavior, we must begin with good treasures in our hearts. It begins with what we focus on. We need to evaluate how much time and commitment we give to focusing on the Word and the kingdom, compared to focusing on what we eat, drink, and wear, etc.

> A good man out of the good treasure of his heart brings forth good things, and an evil man out of the evil treasure brings forth evil things.
> — Matthew 12:35 NKJV

Recap and reflect

- Identify the areas of your heart that are not bringing forth good things and apply the fruit of the Spirit to each area. For example, declare the fruit of the Spirit of peace over your heart if you feel overwhelmed. I call this the Fruit Paradigm, and we will practice more of this as we go along. In the meantime, inspect your heart today.

- Meditate on these verses on fullness: John 17:10–11; Acts 13:52; Romans 15:13; 2 Corinthians 7:4; and Ephesians 1:23, 3:19, 4:10. Write down what life would look like walking in this divine fullness in your heart and soul.

Chapter 11
Focus on the Gift

Scripture references

James 1:17; Genesis 1:31; 1 Timothy 4:3–4; Genesis 2:9; Ecclesiastes 9:7–10; 1 Corinthians 10:31; Revelation 3:20

With Spirit-Full Eating, we want to reignite our thanksgiving and gratitude for the gift that is food. Over the years, we have been so focused on pulling apart foods according to "morals," calories, what nutrients they will give us, and how they will benefit us that we have missed the beauty of the gift.

Initially Adam and Eve probably weren't even thinking much about the tree they were not to eat from. They were probably so busy paying attention to all the beautiful things they could eat. They were focusing on the gifts from their heavenly Father.

> Every good gift and every perfect gift is from above, and comes down from the Father of lights, with whom there is no variation or shadow of turning.
> — James 1:17 NKJV

What they were not allowed to eat was not at the forefront of their minds, until the enemy confused them. But that's what the enemy likes to do—to put the focus on the negative, on things below, on the cares of life, and not on things above.

Let's focus on some truths about the gift that food is:

God created food, and everything He made, He called good.

> And God looked upon all that He had made, and indeed, it
> was very good.
> — Genesis 1:31 NKJV

Paul stated that food created by God is a gift.

> ... abstaining from [certain kinds of] foods which God has
> created to be gratefully shared by those who believe and have
> [a clear] knowledge of the truth. For everything God has
> created is good, and nothing is to be rejected if it is received
> with gratitude; for it is sanctified [set apart, dedicated to
> God] by means of the word of God and prayer.
> — 1 Timothy 4:3–4 AMP

God created food to both look good and be pleasurable.

> And [in that garden] the LORD God caused to grow from the
> ground every tree that is desirable and pleasing to the sight
> and good (suitable, pleasant) for food.
> — Genesis 2:9 AMP

> Go your way, eat your bread with joy, and drink your wine
> with a cheerful heart [if you are righteous, wise, and in the

hands of God]; for God has already approved and accepted
your works.
— Ecclesiastes 9:7–10 AMP

God wants us to come into an eating experience as a form
of worship to God, one where we glorify Him with what we
eat and drink.

So then, whether you eat or drink or whatever you do, do all
to the glory of [our great] God.
— 1 Corinthians 10:31 AMP

Behold, I stand at the door and knock; if anyone hears My
voice and opens the door, I will come into him and will dine
with him, and he with Me.
— Revelation 3:20 NKJV

A meal is promised us in the new heaven and the new
earth.

"Blessed are those who are invited to the marriage supper of
the Lamb." And he said to me, "These are true words of God."
— Revelation 19:9 NKJV

We do not worship the food, but we experience gratitude
to God as the One who provided this great gift. This is the
same as when you go out and admire beautiful scenery, where
you see nature and creation that show the goodness of God.
The Bible says no one has an excuse not to believe because all
we have to do is look out the window and see God's hand. In
the same way, He has blessed us with His food creation.

Paul instructs us not to reject or despise food, but to receive it with thanksgiving and prayer. So, when God gives us a gift, we're meant to use it. This includes using food to serve one another and to show His manifold grace and generosity.

The ministry of food

Eating food is one of the ways we experience the goodness of God. It is to experience how wonderful He is through what He's provided for us. I have had the honor of practicing feasting with Jesus (which we will teach on later in this series) and I have experienced God's nature in my foods.

I have experienced God ministering to my heart through His gift of food. While doing so, I received a revelation that is recorded in one of my conversations with God.

My conversation with God

Lord, now when I see the wonder of Your food, I see the wonder of Your creation—how You have infused Yourself into food; how it was birthed and came from the inner core of who You are. You are showing me that with food, when we eat it, we are truly eating and drinking of the wonder of Your nature and Your character. We get to discover who You are in the food when we cook the food and when we present the food with joy before You.

I thank You that we bless it, make it holy, sanctify, and set it apart. When we take time to sanctify and set it apart, we honor You, and discover You. We're discovering who You are in how You infused Your very nature and being into food and drink. And this is how we partake of this worthily, and this is also how we partake while giving You glory: We recognize that it is Your glory infused into it.

Now I don't want to eat in any form or any way that rejects the gift of God, for to reject it means to despise it. Despising means to see something as small or inconsequential in value, therefore treating it with ineligibility when we don't give it its full attention that it is due.

And I see now why You spoke to me about when we eat; it's about giving food its full attention, but I didn't realize it's actually giving attention to You.

It's a total place of loving You. I get to discover food as You've created it, and it's like delighting in Your creation, mighty hands, soft hands, and creative hands all at the same time.

Thank You, God, for all the food You have made and the ways You have expressed Yourself as an extraordinary artist through food. I repent of treating food as something to be used and abused to reach some weird goal the world has set up and framed. In that I missed You.

I know I have discovered Your truth, and I have discovered who You are. Still, now, I want to spend the rest of my days and the rest of my life seeing food and drink in their rightful place—just as in creation everything points to You. It points to Your goodness. It points to Your love. It points to Your faithfulness. It points to Your self-control. It points to Your gentleness. It points to Your patience, and it points to Your joy.

I'm in love with You, God. I'm in love with You, God. Nothing compares. Nothing can compare to Your goodness. So, Father, even now, I don't even want to eat food unless I can eat it worthily, only before You, in a way that gives You honor, and in a way that I can truly appreciate the gift of God. Oh, there will be no more rejecting of the food gifts that You so lovingly provide, as every gift comes from heaven.

There's no shadow, no variance, and I say yes.

I need to put this in my diary as an appointment with You, Jesus, where I get to come and sit with You and in You, and we get to commune. I get to commune with my family, and I get to rediscover Your beauty. Your wonder, Your all.

In the latter days, we will tremble at Your goodness and wonder. All I want to be is in Your creation. I can sip the slightest bit of kombucha, roll it around my tongue and discover so much about You in that place. I don't want to do anything without thinking of You and what You've done and created. May other people catch this rich, decadent vision of You, and may I be a vessel to help show the revelation of our food, of Your food, and the revelation of You in food.

Creation speaks and teaches!

What about food God never made?

In my days of struggle and obsession with clean eating and trusting God for my eating and drinking, I had a problem with foods that were not found in nature—the packaged and processed foods we are taught are evil, cancer-causing, and death in a box.

What about the foods God didn't make? My answer is simple. God didn't create cars, nor did He create planes, nor did He create the bathtub or shower you use to wash in. He didn't make the paper money or coins in your pocket.

And are there foods God didn't make? Sure! However, they serve their purpose. A homeless and hungry man doesn't care whether your bread is Ezekiel, gluten-free, sourdough, white, or brown. A homeless and thirsty woman doesn't care whether your water is reverse osmosis, via a filter, or from a tap.

Are there foods and drinks that are more beneficial? Yes! But each type of food serves a purpose. God will lead you in what is best, beneficial, and helpful, and what to enjoy in every passing season of life. Our goal is not to be mastered!

Know that God created man in His image and created us to enjoy food! We want to cultivate the desire to enjoy the richness of God's creation, and to see and experience Him in all our meals. Whatever you eat or drink, do it for the glory of the Lord. We are open to hearing the Lord's teaching and training from this place. I encourage you to find the Lord amid any food you eat and, if not, may it be a place to be grateful for the Lord's provision or the company you share as you feast.

The Bible says that it is the truth that you know that sets you free, not merely the truth that you have. So, you can be aware of the truth, continue to walk toward deception, and eventually be mastered by the problem—unless you *know* the truth.

Many of us have built up layers of strongholds over the years. We will see lasting freedom from these strongholds in our souls when we truly know the truth, renew our minds, pull down every lie, and stand in the truth of God's Word. The truth must permeate every part of us—from our perceptions about life to our belief systems and, then, follow through to our actions.

A testimony

(Name withheld for privacy.)

Spirit-Full Eating and living in wholeness is when my spirit, soul, and body are aligned. My spirit and soul form such a strong partnership, and the body does what it sees them doing. I am so in love with Jesus that I enjoy pleasing Him—love-based obedience. My mind is so focused on the Lord that even in a crowded airport, I can have communion with Him.

My actions are a manifestation of what is in my heart. I no longer have a mental obsession with food and with weight control. I no longer live with guilt and shame twenty-four hours a day. I wake up excited to spend time with the Lord.

This is a transformation in my life. I am being sensitive to anything that feels restrictive and going in the other direction. I don't eat crazily or eat everything in sight, and I am grateful.

I love the freedom of eating with my family and not having that constant dialogue in my head: "I want to have this, but I should have that." I can leave food on my plate. Yesterday I didn't eat a quarter of a burger and a third of my fries—it was such a great feeling, and this has never happened before.

I never exercised during my three years in an eating program. My sponsor didn't recommend it, and there seemed to be a sense of pride that you could lose weight without exercising—and I did. Now I want to exercise. After studying the woman described in Proverbs 31, I am inspired to be stronger physically and to have the stamina to do the work I need to do. God is changing my desires.

Recap and reflect

- We are grateful for the gift of food God gave us. We have spent so long dissecting foods that we have missed the gift that food is. We are reconnecting with and reestablishing God's intention for us regarding food. Is it refreshing to now accept His gift? Receive it today with thanksgiving.

- We recognize every gift from God is from our Father of light, for our pleasure and delight, and for its goodness to bless our bodies. Meditate on God's original design for food.

- God wants us to come into a rich eating–worship experience with Him as we feast and sit at the Lord's table. Can you imagine the marriage supper of the lamb described in Revelation?

- We do not worship food. We are not mastered by food, but as all of the creation ministers to the glorious, marvelous hand of Jesus, we open our hearts to His ministry at His table. Take time today to have one meal with the Holy Spirit, and to express gratitude for what's on your plate.

- I shared how we acknowledge that not all foods are the same. Not all foods are 100 percent pure, and clean, and from the ground, but we can find God's handprint in those foods, and in those whom we are blessed to dine with and serve. Can you see it? Can you find God's handprint? Let Him minister to your heart today.

Conclusion

In the pages of this book, we embark on a transformative journey, delving into the essence of Spirit-Full Eating. We discover the foundation for our exploration, highlighting the need to end the endless struggle with weight, body image, false identities, and dieting.

We learn that the true answer lies in completely trusting God for our health and weight concerns, giving Him all the glory. Christ is revealed as the ultimate solution, and living under the guidance of the Holy Spirit leads us each to a personalized plan.

The heart of the book is anchored in 3 John 1:2, where we discover that prosperity in health is intricately linked to the soul prospering. Through the application of the Holy Spirit's strategy for total health, we embark on a path of divine healing.

This journey of Spirit-Full Eating is not about following diets or secular wellness plans, but about surrendering to the Holy Spirit's guidance. The focus is on giving God all the glory as we rebuild His temple —our bodies—and embrace divine health.

Spirit-Full Eating introduces us to reconnecting with the Holy Spirit's leadership, flowing from our spirits to our souls and bodies. We learn the importance of internal transformation, and how seeking health solutions within Christ's will is paramount.

By setting our minds on Christ and seeking His kingdom first, we turn away from anxieties and worries about food and body image, and embrace the simplicity found in Christ. We discover the abundance of wisdom and direction found in dining with Him through His Word.

Our struggles and false attempts remind us that this battle is spiritual, and cannot be solely resolved by willpower or programs. Restriction leads to a rebound effect, emphasizing the need to address the condition of our hearts, souls, and minds for lasting health and prosperity.

We unmask the master distracter, Satan, and his efforts from the beginning to distort our views of God and of food. We recognize the importance of entrusting our hearts to the Lord, breaking free from wrong doctrines, and surrendering to God to rebuild our thoughts with His truth.

We are alert to Satan's schemes to divert us from fulfilling God's plan for our lives. This reminds us of the negative impact of worldly obsessions. It urges us to seek wisdom from God and to focus on fulfilling His calling and mission in our lives. We stand in steadfast prayers of repentance, reaffirming our commitment to remain focused on God's heart, truth, and way.

It is imperative that we pay attention to the voice of the Holy Spirit and guard our hearts against deceiving spirits and the doctrines of demons. The key message is to prioritize our relationship with Christ, to avoid legalistic rules and food restrictions, and to instead love God with all our hearts, souls, and minds.

We are on a mission called "The Great Takeback" where we are taking back what the enemy has stolen and walking in our God-given authority to restore right beliefs about food and our bodies. We find fullness and freedom in Christ. We recognize the abundance He provides, and can therefore focus on walking in our true identities to heal and transform our souls.

We now know the keys to experiencing the fullness of God flowing through our souls. By using the power of imagination, giving thanks, cultivating a heart of worship, and prioritizing the condition of our hearts, we can embrace the fullness of God's plans for our lives.

Hallelujah! We get to focus on the gifts of God. Gratitude and true thanksgiving for the gift of food are so important. Let's see eating as an act of worship and appreciate the beauty of God's provision in every type of food. May we reflect on

God's handprint in all foods, and so receive His ministry to our hearts through feasting with Jesus.

We look forward to *Part Two: Standing Strong,* where we will be equipped with critical tools and mindsets to remain steadfast in our Spirit-Full Eating journeys. Let's continue to embrace divine health through an intimate connection with the Holy Spirit and God's Word, and so experience lasting freedom in Christ.

In conclusion, Spirit-Full Eating is not just about food; it is a journey of spiritual transformation, leading us to the heart of God. As we trust in His guidance, surrender our desires to Him, and embrace divine health, we can stand strong in the middle of the challenges life presents. Let us continue with expectation and surrender, knowing that Christ is the answer and Spirit-Full Eating is the pathway to a life of wholeness, prosperity, and fulfillment in Him.

He is the way, the truth, and the life!

Additional Information

Links to our resources

- www.Spiritfulleating.com Visit this website for resources, blog posts, and further details on Spirit-Full Eating.

- www.facebook.com/spiritfulleating Follow our Spirit-Full Eating Facebook page for updates, tips, help, and encouragement.

- www.tapestryofbeautyministries.com On this website you will learn about Tapestry of Beauty Ministries, the ministry home of Spirit-Full Eating, and our other upcoming studies.

- www.facebook.com/groups/TapestryBeauty Join our Tapestry of Beauty Ministries Facebook group, and discover a like-minded community of women who are on this same journey of finding freedom and renewing their minds.

- www.mindrenewalschool.com This is our Bible school where you can complete our Spirit-Full Eating Bible studies and other programs to help you on your journey.

Further reading on rebounds after restriction

- https://www.ncbi.nlm.nih.gov/pmc/articles/PMC269456 9/

- https://www.sciencedirect.com/science/article/abs/pii/S0 531556513000831?via%3Dihub

- https://www.ncbi.nlm.nih.gov/pmc/articles/PMC223590 7/

If you have any questions, please email us at
team@tapestryofbeautyministries.com.

Disclaimer

The information and material presented in this book, or any Tapestry of Beauty Ministries program, or online teachings may give reference to diets, or programs, or organizations, but this is for the sole purpose of giving an overall understanding of various viewpoints. Each person is responsible for coming to their own conclusion.

We, the Tapestry of Beauty Ministries authors, teachers, presenters, and trainers are in no way responsible or liable for the application of the material. This is the work of every individual believer and their yielding to the Holy Spirit and to God's living Word.

All information presented is not to be construed as medical advice, nor as instruction on activities concerning medicines or medical treatment.

All that is shared comes from a place of compassion and mercy.

Made in the USA
Monee, IL
23 August 2023

670872bb-ded6-4c88-9a10-b827d09a0e7bR01